Banned Books

by Marcia Amidon Lusted

Content Consultant
Paula Rabinowitz
Professor of English
University of Minnesota

CORE
LIBRARY

Published by ABDO Publishing Company, PO Box 398166, Minneapolis, MN 55439. Copyright © 2013 by Abdo Consulting Group, Inc. International copyrights reserved in all countries. No part of this book may be reproduced in any form without written permission from the publisher. The Core Library™ is a trademark and logo of ABDO Publishing Company.

Printed in the United States of America,
North Mankato, Minnesota
112012
012013
♻ THIS BOOK CONTAINS AT LEAST 10% RECYCLED MATERIALS.

Editor: Karen Latchana Kenney
Series Designer: Becky Daum

Cataloging-in-Publication Data
Lusted, Marcia Amidon.
 Banned books / Marcia Amidon Lusted.
   p. cm. -- (Hot topics in media)
Includes index.
ISBN 978-1-61783-731-9
1. Censorship--Juvenile literature. 2. Prohibited book--Juvenile literature.
I. Title.
363.31--dc14

                                    2012946384

Photo Credits: Sherwin McGehee/iStockphoto, cover, 1; AP Images, 4; G. Marshall Wilson/ Ebony Collection/AP Images, 6; UIG/Getty Images, 12; Universal History Archive/Getty Images, 14; Library of Congress, 17; Clark Jones/AP Images, 20; Ron Edmonds/AP Images, 23; Jeff Gentner/ AP Images, 26; The Gadsden Times, Marc Golden/AP Images, 28; Nate Parsons/The Washington Post/Getty Images, 31; Neil Jacobs/Getty Images, 34; Jacek Chabraszewski/Shutterstock Images, 36, 45; Monkey Business Images/Shutterstock Images, 41

CONTENTS

SLAUGHTERHOUSE-FIVE   KURT VONNEGUT, JR.

SOUL ON ICE   ELDRIDGE CLEAVER

THE NAKED APE   DESMOND MORRIS

Go Ask Alice   Anonymous

DOWN THESE MEAN STREETS · PIRI THOMAS

WNEV

CHAPTER ONE

Book Banning Goes to Court

In 1976 17-year-old student Steven Pico was angry. He had just learned that the board of education for his high school's district had decided to remove some books from his school library. Nine books would no longer be available for students to check out and read.

Why would the school board do this? Several board members of the Island Trees Union Free School

Author Kurt Vonnegut Jr. spoke to reporters on October 3, 1980, about the school board ban of a number of books, including his *Slaughterhouse Five*.

A book written by author Alice Childress was banned by the school board at Steven's school.

District in New York had gone to a conference and heard a presentation by the group Parents of New York United (PONYU). This was a group that worried about education in the state and had conservative political views. The group created a list of books that they felt were objectionable to children because of content the PONYU considered to be anti-American, anti-religious, and obscene.

The school board members returned to the school building that night after students and teachers were gone. They found nine books from the PONYU list and decided to take the books off the shelves. They put the books in the board's office where only the board members could read and evaluate them.

Later the school board appointed a committee of parents and teachers to read the books. The committee recommended that several of the books go back in the library. But the school board rejected the committee's opinion. The board kept the nine books off the shelves.

The Removed Books

The books removed from the library shelves at the Island Trees High School were:

- *Slaughterhouse-Five* by Kurt Vonnegut
- *The Fixer* by Bernard Malamud
- *The Naked Ape* by Desmond Morris
- *Down These Mean Streets* by Piri Thomas
- *Best Short Stories of Negro Writers*, edited by Langston Hughes
- *Go Ask Alice* by Anonymous
- *Laughing Boy* by Oliver LaFarge
- *Black Boy* by Richard Wright
- *A Hero Ain't Nothing But a Sandwich* by Alice Childress
- *Soul on Ice* by Eldridge Cleaver

It's My Right to Read

Steven Pico, three of his high school friends, and a junior high student sued the school board for denying their First Amendment rights. That amendment deals with freedom of speech and the press. Steven and his friends felt that when the school board banned the books, it blocked their right to a free press. This included being able to read what they wanted to read.

The case went to several courts. The US

Supreme Court made the final decision on the case on June 25, 1982. It ruled in favor of the students. It decided that the right to access books was part of the First Amendment. The Court also noted that local school boards were not allowed to take books from school library shelves simply because they did not like the ideas in those books.

Just the Beginning

Steven Pico and his friends won their case. The Supreme Court's ruling has been used to decide other similar cases. But book banning continues. In fact, every year there are hundreds of cases of parents or community members who voice concerns about books and demand that they be removed from libraries. Sometimes books are simply challenged. That means that someone tries to get the books removed from the library. Other times books are banned. That means that books have been removed.

Do all books belong in a school or community library? This is a question that often makes people angry or upset. Some feel their right to free speech is being taken away if a book is removed from public access. But some want more control over what their children read. Book banning occurs frequently. The issue itself is not new. It has been taking place for as long as there have been books.

This is an excerpt from the US Supreme Court ruling in the *Board of Education, Island Trees Union Free School District v Pico:*

> *A school library, no less than any other public library, is "a place dedicated to quiet, to knowledge, and to beauty." As one District Court has well put it, in the school library "a student can literally explore the unknown, and discover areas of interest and thought not covered by the prescribed curriculum. . . . [The] student learns that a library is a place to test or expand upon ideas presented to him, in or out of the classroom."*

Source: Board of Education, Island Trees Union Free School District v. Pico 457 US 853. Supreme Court of US. 1982. Legal Information Institute. Cornell University Law School, n.d. Web. Accessed October 17, 2012.

What's the Big Idea?

Take a close look at the court's ruling. What is the main idea? What evidence is used to support the court's point? Come up with a few sentences showing how the court's ruling uses two or three pieces of evidence to support the main point.

CHAPTER TWO

A History of Book Banning

Around 350 BCE in ancient Greece, the philosopher Plato suggested that certain fables and legends should not be told to children. The first books had to be printed by hand. It took a very long time to make books. They were extremely valuable and precious. If someone objected to the contents of a book, it was much easier to find the copies, burn them, and destroy the book forever.

German printer Johannes Gutenberg's printing press changed the way books were printed, making them harder to destroy forever.

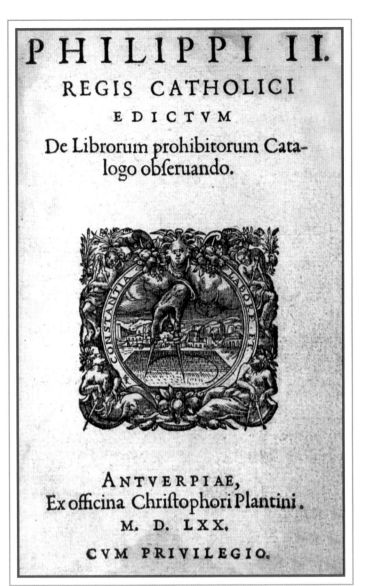

The Roman Catholic Church's *Index Librorum Prohibitorum* listed banned books for almost 400 years.

Johannes Gutenberg invented the printing press in the 1300s in Germany. It suddenly made it much cheaper and easier to make many copies of a single book. More books could be shared with more people.

It also meant that burning a book no longer destroyed it forever.

England created a system where printers had to get permission from the Church of England before they could publish a manuscript. In 1559 the Roman Catholic Church published its first list of forbidden books. The books listed were thought to be immoral or contain errors about religion. The list was called the *Index Librorum Prohibitorum*. It contained a guideline for censors to use in granting or denying printers permission to publish books. The *Index Librorum Prohibitorum* continued to be compiled and published for almost 400 years until 1966. It grew to be more than 5,000 titles long.

The *Index*

The 1559 *Index Librorum Prohibitorum* banned books by Protestant leaders, such as Martin Luther. Other religious books, such as the Koran and the Talmud, were also banned. Some works by philosophers Plato, Aristotle, and Homer were banned because passages went against Roman Catholic teachings.

Book Banning in America

One of the first book burnings in the American colonies took place in 1650. The General Court of the Massachusetts Bay Colony banned a religious pamphlet called *The Meritorious Price of Our Redemption* by William Pynchon. This pamphlet went against the Puritan religion of the time. It was gathered and publicly burned in Boston.

However, one of the most famous censors in the United States was Anthony Comstock. He founded a group called the New York Society for the Suppression of Vice in 1872. A vice is a bad habit, such as excessive

Questioning the Comstock Law

A series of Nazi book burnings in 1933 made people question the Comstock Law. People were frightened to see the public events of burning books. Soon after, the court case *United States v. One Book Called* Ulysses challenged a book ban. This case looked at the ban on *Ulysses* and the court ruled that the book was not obscene. Because of the ruling, it could no longer be banned.

Anthony Comstock worked to ban books he believed were obscene.

drinking. Part of Comstock's goal was to ban books that had any content that he considered to be filthy, obscene, or indecent. Comstock persuaded the US Congress to pass a law in 1873. It was known as the Comstock Law. It banned the mailing of any indecent materials, including books. It also influenced the creation of similar laws.

Between the years 1874 and 1915, Comstock was an official for the US Postal Service. During that time, the law allowed an estimated 160 tons (109 metric tons) of printed material to be confiscated. This included books such as *The Arabian Nights*, as well as those by authors Ernest Hemingway, F. Scott Fitzgerald, and John Steinbeck. The law and other similar laws were later relaxed.

Invisible Censorship

Today, books are sometimes banned in more subtle ways. If a librarian feels that having a certain book on the shelf might create controversy, he or she may decide not to order that book at all. This invisible censorship keeps certain titles from being available to library patrons and students.

In 1860 a pamphlet written by John Stuart Mill was published. It was titled *On Liberty*. Mill discussed the dangers of silencing opinions. He wrote:

> *But the peculiar evil of silencing the expression of an opinion is, that it is robbing the human race; posterity as well as the existing generation; those who dissent from the opinion, still more than those who hold it. If the opinion is right, they are deprived of the opportunity of exchanging error for truth: if wrong, they lose, what is almost as great a benefit, the clearer perception and livelier impression of truth, produced by its collision with error.*

> *Source: Mill, John Stuart. On Liberty. Project Gutenberg. January 10, 2011. Web. Accessed September 22, 2012.*

What's the Big Idea?

Take a close look at Mill's words. What is his main idea? What evidence does he use to support his point? Come up with a short paragraph showing how Mill uses two or three pieces of evidence to support a main point.

CHAPTER THREE

Why Are Books Banned?

The Harry Potter Series is one of the most popular book series for kids. The seven books in the series are about a boy wizard named Harry Potter. Many people feel the books have a positive message about friendship, loyalty, and doing what is right. The plots are exciting too. This helps make the books appealing to many kids.

Young fans hold their new Harry Potter books at a book release party in 2007.

The Harry Potter books are also the most frequently banned books of the last 15 years. Why? Some people feel that magic and wizardry are themes that kids should not read about. Some religious groups feel that these books steer children away from God and the church.

Reasons for Banning

The controversy about the Harry Potter books is one example of why books are banned. In this case, some people were strongly against the books for religious reasons. But there are other reasons why books are often challenged or banned.

The Satanic Verses

In September 1988, author Salman Rushdie's novel *The Satanic Verses* was published. Some Muslim religious leaders thought the book was offensive to their religion. Iran's religious leader issued a *fatwa* (a religious order) calling for Rushdie's death. He went into hiding. Stores that sold his book were bombed. Some people who helped translate the novel were injured or killed. The order for Rushdie's death is still in place and was reaffirmed by another Islamic leader, Ayatollah Ali Khamenei, in 2005.

Author Salman Rushdie spoke at a conference in 1992.

Many books written for teens have realistic portrayals of sexual encounters and sexual feelings. There can sometimes be similar issues with adult books as well.

People also challenge books for political reasons. In countries where citizens are tightly controlled by their government, books may be challenged, banned, or even burned as a way to keep revolutionary ideas away from the general public.

Books can also be banned for social reasons. In countries where Islamic extremists do not believe that girls should be educated, books have been burned in girls' schools. Books that might create social tension

Naked *In The Night Kitchen*

The picture book *In the Night Kitchen* was written and illustrated by Maurice Sendak. It is frequently challenged in elementary schools. Why? The three-year-old main character, Mickey, appears totally naked in several of the book's illustrations. Many people find any type of nudity in books to be unacceptable. They seek to remove books with even illustrated nudity from library shelves.

might be challenged. And books that might make people question the way things are in their society can also be placed on banned lists by their governments.

People sometimes object to certain language in a book. The use of profanity or violence can cause conflict. Some might object to the family situation presented in the story, such as same-sex couples and their families. Some people may have concerns about a book because of a certain illustration, especially if it portrays nudity.

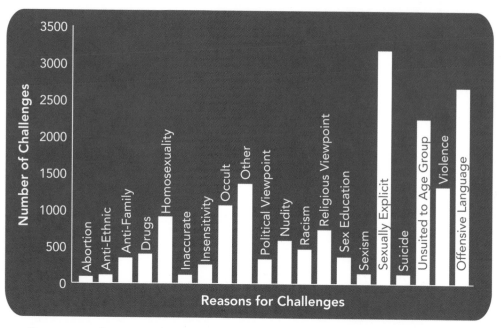

Reasons for Book Challenges

This chart shows some of the reasons why books were challenged from 1990–2010. How does the chart visually explain information that is in the text? How is the chart's information different from the text? Does it convey the same or different information?

The Process of Challenging

How does a book become challenged and then banned? It can happen in several ways. A book is published and someone reads it. The person finds something objectionable about it. That person could be a parent reading something that a child has brought home from school or the library. That person

George Washington High School student Makenzie Hatfield holds books that were banned at her school.

could be a member of a religious group reading a book that shocks and upsets the group.

Most often, people simply refuse to read the book or decide not to allow their children to read it. But some people may take the next step of challenging the book. The group or person then warns parents or other group members not to read a certain book. The issue may then be brought up with a teacher, principal, or a school board. The person may then ask that the book be removed from the school library.

Most school boards and school districts now have rules in place for dealing with book challenges. This usually involves a review of the book by a panel of teachers, administrators, and parents. The school board can hold hearings where members of the public can speak for both sides. Finally, the district will make a ruling about whether to remove a book from its shelves, leave it alone, or start a policy where parents have to sign a permission slip before their child can read the book.

CHAPTER FOUR

The Fight Over Book Banning

Book banning often brings people with different values into direct conflict with each other. It also shows just how powerful people believe books are.

One of the most visible organizations concerned about book banning is the American Library Association (ALA). Every year the ALA sponsors Banned Books Week to highlight the issue. The ALA

A banned books display was set up at the Gadsden Public Library in Gadsden, Alabama, to recognize the American Library Association's Banned Books Week in 2009.

2011's Banned Books

According to the ALA, the top ten most frequently challenged books were:

- ttyl; ttfn; l8r, g8r (series) by Lauren Myracle
- The Color of Earth (series) by Kim Dong Hwa
- The Hunger Games trilogy by Suzanne Collins
- *My Mom's Having a Baby!: A Kid's Month-by-Month Guide to Pregnancy* by Dori Hillestad Butler
- *The Absolutely True Diary of a Part-Time Indian* by Sherman Alexie
- Alice (series) by Phyllis Reynolds Naylor
- *Brave New World* by Aldous Huxley
- *What My Mother Doesn't Know* by Sonya Sones
- Gossip Girl (series) by Cecily von Ziegesar
- *To Kill a Mockingbird* by Harper Lee

also publishes a list of that year's most frequently challenged or banned books. The ALA believes that Banned Books Week celebrates the freedom to read, the importance of the First Amendment, and the benefits of free access to information. It also highlights the negative aspects of censorship.

But some are opposed to Banned Books Week. They feel it supports a system in which there is no control over what children read. Book banning is often considered to be

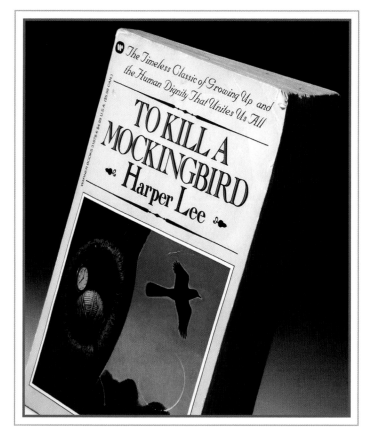

Harper Lee's novel portrays race relations in the southern United States during the 1930s.

unacceptable in US culture. Book banning opponents argue that many times a book hasn't even been read by those who challenge it.

A Matter of Timing

Book banning may reflect a certain time and place in history. Many books that have been banned are

To Kill a Mockingbird

One of the most banned books in the United States is *To Kill a Mockingbird* by Harper Lee. Her only published novel was released in 1960. At the time, the Civil Rights Movement was happening in the United States. The legacy of slavery and racism continue to be powerful forces in the United States. Her book openly discussed those issues. In 1961, Lee was awarded the Pulitzer Prize for her book. It was also made into a movie.

considered to be literary classics by others. This includes books such as Mark Twain's *Huckleberry Finn* and Harper Lee's *To Kill a Mockingbird*. Both books contain language that is considered racist today, but both represent life as it was during certain times in US history. The general views of society are constantly changing. Many books that were considered obscene at one time are thought to be tame now.

The fear that parents may challenge a book can influence what a teacher assigns for a class to read. A teacher has a huge responsibility in a classroom. He or she provides information to students. How should a teacher choose that information? People have a right to protest books they don't like. But do they have the right to impose their choices on others? This is one big issue with banning books.

Fighting over Harry

The censorship of the Harry Potter books is a good example of how book banning can make people choose sides. The two sides came into conflict in 1999 during an attempt to censor the Harry Potter books in the school district of Zeeland, Michigan. The school superintendent sent out a memo restricting the availability of the books in town schools. Students in the school district were angry at the ruling. They created the Web site *Muggles for Harry Potter*. It was a tool to pressure the school board to allow the books back into the schools. Soon more than 18,000 people across the country registered on the Web site. They wanted to help fight censorship in the school district.

A copy of a Harry Potter book burns in a bonfire outside Christ Community Church on December 30, 2001, in Alamogordo, New Mexico.

Many of the books' challengers received support from all over the country as well. Christ Community Church in Alamogordo, New Mexico, sponsored a book burning in December of 2001. Copies of Harry Potter books, books by Stephen King, and some movies and music were burned in a large bonfire. In the end, though, the Zeeland decision was reversed.

Most people agree that people have a right to not read a book that they find offensive. But should one group have the power to tell other people what they can and cannot read?

EXPLORE ONLINE

The focus in Chapter Four was the conflicts with book banning. It also touched upon the fight over the Harry Potter books in Zeeland, Michigan. The Web site below focuses on the fight in Zeeland. As you know, every source is different. How is the information given in the Web site different from the information in this chapter? What information is the same? How do the two sources present information differently? What can you learn from this Web site?

Fight for Harry Potter!
www.kidspeakonline.org/fighthp_zeeland.html

CHAPTER FIVE

Challenging Books Today

The content of books continues to be an issue in schools. In 2011 the ALA reported that 326 books were challenged in schools that year. Restricting children's access to a book often serves to make that book more attractive to kids. Even in the adult world, books that stir up controversy often sell better because of that publicity. Many people challenge books wanting to protect their children and

When a book is banned from a library, it affects the choices readers can make about what to read.

uphold certain values. But other people may not want those choices made for their own children, particularly if they don't agree with the reasons. Many book banning incidents become large-scale legal battles. They involve people's views on freedom of speech and access to information. Books have been challenged in many states around the country. It is a controversy that is seen across the United States.

The Future of Book Banning

Challenging and banning books may become more difficult in the digital age. Parents may find it harder to keep books that they

Even in Fairy Tales

One of the most familiar fairy tales that kids hear is *Little Red Riding Hood*. It is the story of a little girl who goes to visit her grandmother and barely escapes a wolf that tries to eat her. The school board in Empire, California, challenged a book containing a traditional version of *Little Red Riding Hood* in 1990. In the original story, Little Red Riding Hood brings a bottle of wine to her sick grandmother. The school board thought that this would encourage children to drink alcohol.

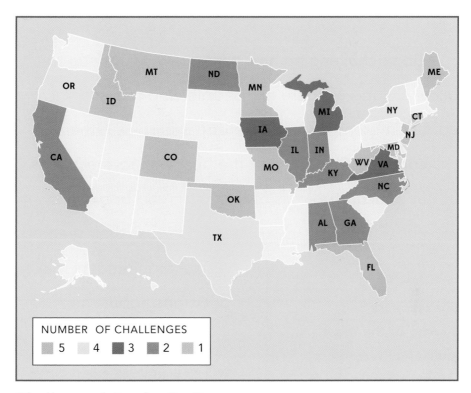

NUMBER OF CHALLENGES
5   4   3   2   1

Challenged Books By State

This map shows the number of books that were challenged in different states from December 2006 to May 2009. How does the map visually explain information that is in the text? How is the map's information different from the text? How is it similar?

don't approve of out of their children's hands. With the instant availability of e-books and other digital editions, books are more easily accessed than ever before. Many classic books are now available for free on the Internet. And books can be purchased at both physical and online bookstores.

Book challenging and banning will continue to occur as long as there are people who feel strongly about different issues presented in books. Others will continue to claim that the best way to teach kids about difficult topics is to let them read books and then discuss their reading with them. Readers make decisions about the information they will or will not access each time they read a book. This choice is at the heart of the book banning debate.

Bowdlerized!

William Shakespeare's plays are some of the most cherished classic literature of all time. Most students study them in school. But in 1818, Thomas Bowdler published a version of Shakespeare's plays that had been edited for family reading. He took out love scenes and any language he thought was offensive. Today when something is censored because of its supposed inappropriate content, it is said to be *bowdlerized*.

School libraries are filled with information for students to access.

IMPORTANT DATES

350 BCE

Greek philosopher Plato suggests that certain fables should not be told to children.

1559 CE

The Roman Catholic Church publishes its first list of forbidden books.

1650

The Massachusetts Bay Colony bans the religious pamphlet *The Meritorious Price of Our Redemption* by William Pynchon.

1976

Nine books are removed from Steven Pico's school library by the school board.

1982

In June, the US Supreme Court rules in favor of students in the case of *Board of Education, Island Trees Union Free School District v Pico*.

1988

Salman Rushdie's novel *The Satanic Verses* is published, offending some Muslim leaders.

1818

Thomas Bowdler publishes a version of Shakespeare's plays with certain content removed.

1873

The Comstock Law passes and bans the mailing of indecent materials, including books.

1933

Nazis in Germany burn thousands of books in a series of huge bonfires.

1999

A school district in Zeeland, Michigan, bans the Harry Potter books from school libraries.

2001

Christ Community Church in Alamogordo, New Mexico, has a book burning in which Harry Potter and Stephen King books are burned.

2011

The ALA reports that 326 books were challenged.

STOP AND THINK

Why Do I Care?

This book explains how book banning affects readers. List two or three ways that you think book banning has affected your life. For example, pretend a book has been banned from your school. What steps do you take after the ban?

Another View

There are many sources online and in your library about book banning. Ask a librarian or other adult to help you find a reliable source on book banning. Compare what you learn in this new source and what you have found out in this book. Then write a short essay comparing and contrasting the new source's view of book banning to the ideas in this book. How are they different? How are they similar? Why do you think they are different or similar?

Surprise Me

The history of book banning can be interesting and surprising. What two or three facts were most interesting or surprising to you? Write a few sentences about each fact. Why did you find each to be interesting or surprising?

Say What?

Studying book banning can mean learning a lot of new vocabulary. Find five words in this book you've never seen or heard before. Use a dictionary to find out what they mean. Then write the meanings in your own words, and use each word in a new sentence.

GLOSSARY

amendment
a change that is made to a law or a legal document

censorship
taking out parts of a book or other type of media that is thought to be harmful or offensive to the public

confiscate
take something away because it is no longer allowed

conservative
holding to traditional values and cautious about change

controversy
an issue that causes an argument

immoral
going against what is generally accepted as right

objectionable
unpleasant or offensive

obscene
offensive by certain standards of morality

pamphlet
a small, thin book or publication

Puritan
a member of an English religious group in the 1500s and 1600s with strict moral beliefs

LEARN MORE

Books

Barbour, Scott. *Censorship: Opposing Viewpoints.* Farmington Hills, MI: Greenhaven Press, 2010.

Burns, Kate. *Fighters Against Censorship: History Makers.* Farmington Hills, MI: Lucent Books, 2003.

Madden, Kerry. *Harper Lee: A Twentieth-Century Life.* New York: Viking, 2009.

Web Links

To learn more about banned books, visit ABDO Publishing Company online at **www.abdopublishing.com**. Web sites about banned books are featured on our Book Links page. These links are routinely monitored and updated to provide the most current information available.

Visit **www.mycorelibrary.com** for free additional tools for teachers and students.

INDEX

ABOUT THE AUTHOR

Marcia Amidon Lusted is the author of more than 75 books for young readers, as well as more than 350 magazine articles. She is also an assistant editor for Cobblestone Publishing's six magazines, a writing instructor, and a musician. She lives in New Hampshire.